make room
for good

renuka i

ᵇ**bigg**

LIFE
Inspiration and Personal Growth

This book contains original thoughts inspired by true life events of the author. Any resemblance is purely coincidental.

make room for good

A bbigg Book. Published by bbigg Applications Inc.

PRINTING HISTORY
First Publication, eBook edition: April 2013
Revised paperback edition: November 2020

For information and/or to request permission for distribution, please contact: info@bbiggApps.com

ISBN: 978-0-9917358-3-9 (pbk)

dedication

To my dad, sister and grandparents.

It was while dealing with your loss, that my life took shape and began to grow in beautiful ways.

acknowledgments

To my mom and brother:

God made two of the most remarkable people to put on this earth. And lucky for me – I get to call one my mother, and the other my brother. You never shoot down my dreams; instead you encourage me to dream bigger. It is only because of your support that my words have become something more than mere thoughts in my head. This book exists because you gave me the freedom to create it. I will never forget the sacrifices you have made on my behalf.

To my family:

Anetha K., Anujan K., Angelaa K., Baira R., Gajan Y., Kalpana G., Maathavan T., Matangi T., Nive T., Ravi G., Sabesh B., Sathes B., Suba T., and the remainder of my cousins, aunts and uncles - I didn't choose you, God chose you for me. And I couldn't have asked for a more wonderful group of people to call family. You all, in some way have supported me in this journey called life. Your love is what makes it so easy to follow my dreams.

To my girls:

Erika M., Ghrace J., Idil H., Kim L., Rasheeda A., Sarah S., Seema C. – I know how special our friendship is. I never forget to cherish the rarity of our love. You are the only group of people with whom I can talk to ten times a day and still miss. In your presence alone, I can enjoy the chaos as much as I can enjoy the silence. You protect my heart and soul. You inspire me. You are the reason life is beautiful.

To my boys:

Allykhan S., Asif J., Faizal J. – if only you really knew how much I value our bond. You make me laugh, you make me feel safe. You ground me when my head is too high up in the clouds. And what I love most is that you never ask me to come down - you just let me be. I don't give you enough credit for the things that you do. It's only because there's something beautiful about being able to appreciate you without having to vocalize it.

Areez R., Ashif K., Humdan Y., Jeff K., Justin K., Kabir M., Navi K., Omer S., Zeeshan U. – in a world where guys and girls apparently can't be friends - I have all of you. There is a reason why I make an honest effort to keep in touch with you. At key moments you have been there to remind me that I never have to face life alone. I hope you know how much your friendship means to me.

foreword

Whether it's to combat some form of negativity or simply because we need to believe that life is beautiful, no matter the ups and downs, faith gives us hope to keep going even when we don't see a reason to. Or as Renuka often says, "Everything that's happening to you, is happening for you."

There's something incredibly validating about hearing her words, and knowing that someone has been where you are and is encouraging you to keep trying, to keep hoping and to follow through on your pursuit of happiness - however you define it. What's most inspiring and authentic about her writing is that she doesn't try to discredit or deny experiences that bring about regret or remorse. Instead Renuka encourages you to embrace those moments and live life more fully because of, not in spite of, them.

In poignant words that illustrate wisdom beyond her years, she speaks of the value of vulnerability, of dreaming with your eyes wide open, of seeking wisdom and love. Life often times challenges all of these notions and it is so much easier to give into bitterness, to let that be the mark of a particular experience upon you. I hope you take away from her words what I have time and time again – inspiration and strength in the face of challenges that you find yourself doubting your ability to overcome. Wherever life takes you, this pocketful of perspective will no doubt be a reminder that every step of the way you have reasons to appreciate and celebrate how far you've come and how far you are capable of going.

Nivethika

prologue

I would like to think that I have always been a writer at heart. I 'wrote' my first book at the age of seven. I did it during the free time we were given in class one day while the other children used the time to play. My teacher was so impressed, that she got it published. Of course, by published I mean she took it to the principal's office and had it laminated. Back then, writing to me was in fact an aspect of play. It allowed me to bring my imagination to life. Words were a tool for expression as a child. Little did I know that as an adult, this tool would become the very thing to inject meaning into my life...

It all began when I experienced the loss of my father, sister and grandfather - all of whom died one year apart from one another. I was suddenly catapulted out of my bubble of bliss, and forced to face a foreign world that I did not know how to live in. I was in my early twenties. And at such an age, while my peers were 'finding themselves', I was struggling to come to terms with living a life without half of my family. Saying those were the darkest days of my life would be an understatement. I was fortunate enough to have a support system filled with some of the most loyal, considerate people. It was here that I learned the true meaning of love. In fact, it forever changed the way I looked at love. These special people cushioned the blow. But even they couldn't pull me out of this hole. Given that I was normally a happy person, I didn't feel at home amidst the turmoil. I was drowning, and I was looking for a way out of the troubled waters.

It was then that I put pen to paper and began this life-altering journey. Writing became a cathartic process. Problems always felt resolved when I sorted it out on paper. When debilitating thoughts began to re-surface, I simply re-read what I wrote, and they were immediately put to rest. As the years progressed, my grief taught me how to view life differently; how to think deeply, and how to live as a better human being. It was through these thoughts that my quotes were born. And it wasn't until I shared a few of them on social media, that I realized these quotes were more than just therapy for me alone. Suddenly I had people contacting me, telling me that they looked forward to my inspiring thought of the day - that they were dealing with an issue and found exactly what they needed to hear in my quotes – that they wanted to know how I managed to read their minds and put their thoughts into words.

If I have inspired even one of you; helped to uplift your day; prompted you to think about life for even just a moment – then this labour of love has been entirely worth it. My words reflect a life of loss, love and enlightenment. I wanted nothing more than to share this quest – because the growth of one person is of no value unless it can benefit others.

contents

live

love

dream

live

everything happening to you,

is happening for you.

start taking notice
of every simple pleasure around you.
soak it up, no matter how small.
a collection of tiny, happy moments
can be just as good
as a life filled with lavish events.

we think people

who have experienced

very little struggle in life

are the ones who are blessed.

but the people

who have endured difficulties

know a side of life

that can never be taught -

only experienced.

now that, is a blessing.

your nice words don't count
if they're filled with resentment.

life is meant to be bittersweet.

bitter, because the good never lasts.

sweet, because neither does the bad.

pretending to be

happy in life

is not enough for you.

do not fear pain.

it is as much a part of life as joy is.

welcome it,

let it stay for as long as it needs to.

barricading it from coming in

is the reason we can't heal.

some things in life

just aren't worth

waiting around to fix.

get something better

for yourself.

God only gives you
what you're capable of enduring.
but thankfully,
He's also around to intervene
in the moments
when your endurance
runs out of steam.

the more days you spend
yearning for the perfect life
to come along,
the less you have
to find perfection
in the life you lead now.

be in such a good place
that negativity can't survive
in your presence.

your peace
is not allowed
to be interrupted.

there will only ever be

one day like today.

don't spend it thinking about

what you should've done yesterday

or what you could be doing tomorrow.

be present.

when you witness

other people in love,

other people in pain -

remember,

those are lessons for you, too.

if it seems too good to be true,

then maybe it is.

or maybe... it's just that good.

unique people are so accommodating
of another person's uniqueness.
and that's a beautiful thing...
when others make it easy to be you
in this world.

when you're behaving poorly,
catch yourself and stop it,
before someone else
has to point it out to you.
self awareness is an integral part
of being a good person.

every day is a miracle.

and we get to be a part of it.

isn't that something?

happiness is not something

only the elite have access to.

it's attainable, and you can have it -

all you have to do

is choose it for yourself.

if you can't be yourself
around them,
those people
aren't meant for you.

you are right where

you need to be in this moment.

stop worrying.

in a world filled with people

obsessed with extravagance,

it's a refreshing thing

to be simple.

be yourself
and don't apologize for it.
someone else
having a problem with it
is not your problem.

we all have difficult days.

but being rude

should never be an option.

if the rest of us

have to exercise control,

so do you.

you've been bruised.

pain can do that to you.

it's not something

you need to cover up, though.

they are signs

that you've lived

and continue to live.

don't take it personally -
someone else's bad day
has nothing to do with you.
don't let it ruin yours.

when you start to believe

that only good is coming your way,

you'll begin to see every setback

as a breakthrough -

just doing its part

to get you to the good.

happiness is your responsibility.

you cannot depend on others for it.

cultivate your own,

and you never

have to wait again

for someone to provide for you.

at peace in your mind.

at peace in your heart.

imagine how much happier

we would be

if we celebrated small victories

as if they were giant ones?

if negativity is what's taking up space

in your life,

how will you ever have room

for joy?

do you ever wish people would recognize
how wonderful you are?
say to yourself
what you yearn for them to say to you.
we've made the mistake of thinking
we need someone else to validate us.
you don't need to hear it
from another person
to believe it's true.

be happy right now.
you don't need to have
every desire fulfilled
before you can be.
this is
an important lesson to learn.
we don't have to wait for joy.

nobody warned us
that life would involve tragedy.
how beautiful it is
to witness people
who accommodate it
with such elegance.

people who do things

to get a rise out of others,

lack class.

and people who choose

not to react to it,

not to retaliate because of it,

exude class.

did you ever think to be grateful
for what you don't have?
that by not granting it to you,
God is shielding you from a life
that would turn you into someone
you shouldn't be.

go to bed being thankful

for yet another night that we get to

sleep... not everyone makes it through

the day.

wake up thankful

for yet another day that we get to live...

not everyone makes it through the night.

harboring hatred for others

will poison your heart.

don't let awful people

be the reason

your love and kindness

has limitations.

you may not like everyone

you encounter in life,

nor may they like you back.

but that should never stop you

from being civil.

offer as if you have everything

even when you have nothing.

if you're offering
generosity and kindness
in hopes of receiving
something in return,
you're doing it
for the wrong reasons.

what one says holds truth

only if what one does reflects it.

doing what's right
doesn't always act in your favour.
which is why
you should be proud of yourself
each and every time
you choose right over wrong.

be the example -
handle every situation
with integrity.

you can't opt out

of the struggles that you face in life.

but you can change

how you handle them.

live your life with good intentions.
even if you make a mistake,
at least your heart
is in the right place.

you don't know
another person's struggle
enough to judge them.
let's leave that up to God.

choosing not to battle
in order to keep the peace
can be just as rewarding
as going to battle and winning.

may God grant us the strength

to be patient

with the people in this world

who don't always deserve it.

don't let the only perspective

you have on life

be your own.

open your heart.

it's easy

to come up with solutions

to problems

you've never had to endure.

remember this

before you throw in your two cents.

it's never the wrong time
to do the right thing.

envy is ugly.

don't be ugly.

karma reacts to your intentions

behind a good deed –

not the good deed itself.

so if you're offering kindness

with a spiteful heart,

it's unkindness

that you receive in return.

even when life
isn't going well,
you can still find something
to be grateful for.

don't jump to conclusions.

there's a chance that you're wrong.

and even a chance

is a lot of time wasted

on something

that you aren't even certain is true.

sometimes you're going to

question yourself

for choosing to be kind

to those who choose to be cruel.

but no amount of doubt

should ever make you

want to be any other way.

let the pain
you've had to endure
serve you.
use it to help others
make sense of their own pain.
transform it
into something beautiful.

it's not them.

it's you.

stop blaming others

for everything in life

that isn't at its best.

fix yourself first.

ask for what you want.

your other option is to wait

for people to figure it out.

save yourself time,

speak up.

live an endless cycle of good.

do good – receive good.

stop expecting things to go wrong.

not every good thing

is headed for disaster.

let it go.

it may be unfair,

they may be wrong,

you may not deserve it...

even so,

just let it go.

it's a good time to leave behind
everything that doesn't work
for you in life,
and everyone that doesn't work
to be in your life.

bad days don't have to exist.
not because you've stopped
every crappy thing from happening.
but because you've decided
to live in a world
where absolutely nothing
is allowed to ruin your day.

why do bad things happen
to good people?
no one knows.
but you've got to admire
good people -
because even hardships
can't waver
their positive outlook on life.

making mistakes
is part of the journey.
it's the only way
to grow into a better man,
a better woman.
stop punishing yourself
for what you did wrong
in the past.

learning to tolerate

toxic people

is part of being an adult.

also part of being an adult:

keeping them

at arm's length.

how beautiful this world could be,

if everyone was free to be themselves.

and the rest of us protected them.

how you choose

to handle difficult situations

is directly related to your character.

don't behave poorly

and then blame it

on the other people involved.

no one but you

is responsible for your actions.

don't be a slave

to your negative thoughts.

find freedom in optimism.

if you want to know the truth
about someone -
go to the source,
not the grapevine.

just because
a question is asked of you,
doesn't mean
you have to answer it.
save your personal life
for the people
you want to share it with,
not for those
who have no shame in prying.

a woman of class

doesn't believe in revenge.

be grounded in your beliefs.
not everyone
is going to understand them/
agree with them/
accept you because of them.
but none of those
are good enough reasons
for you to give up on them.
stay true to your convictions.

no amount of success
should erase the lessons we learned
while growing up modestly.
when you have nothing, be humble.
when you have everything, be humble.

love

never be afraid to feel.

if you're staring out your window
waiting for 'better' to come along,
you're not going to notice
when the best thing you've ever had
packs their bags
and walks out the door.

don't hurt people

just because they've hurt you.

that takes deliberate hate.

and that's not who you are.

good people are rare.

the most reckless

thing you can do

is have them in your life

and forget how special they are.

friendships are sacred.

the minute you take one for granted,

is the minute

you're no longer deserving of it.

what's meant for you
will always be yours.
if they left,
they'll return.
if you left,
you'll find your way back.

sometimes you need to know
what it feels like to miss it,
so you know
what it feels like to want it back.
and then you'll never forget to cherish
what it feels like to keep it.

pain doesn't disappear overnight.
being there to help someone through it,
shouldn't have a time limit either.
a good friend is there,
even when the issue
has become stale to everyone else.

having the reputation
of being a good person
isn't enough.
don't believe
that title is forever yours,
without you having
to prove it with your actions.

you deserve people
who believe in your worth,
and take time out of their lives
to prove it.

invest in your loved ones.

in the end,

they are all that matter.

not your job, not your money,

not your things.

if you're going to make promises
when you're at your happiest,
make sure you uphold them
when you're at your worst.

life isn't easy.

you learn to handle it.

if only

more people realized

that you didn't have to

do it alone.

go ahead, remember your past.

but only the good parts.

anything else

isn't worth going back for.

it's easy to be faithful.

if it's not easy for you,

you're with the wrong person.

when you know

that what you have

is irreplaceable,

no one better exists.

if you're still thinking about it,

give it a chance.

it hasn't left your mind

for a reason.

talk about your relationships

when they're going well,

not only when they're problematic.

be grateful for

the love that you have.

choose people

that enhance your life.

because in this chosen world,

no one is fake,

no one has ulterior motives,

and no one wants to see you fail.

strong men

have gentle souls.

don't make excuses

for the weak.

that wall you put up

may be good

at keeping out the pain.

but it's also

what's keeping out the love.

life seems more bearable

from the giving or receiving end

of a hug.

you can't separate a person
from their family, their friends,
their belief system.
none of it will ever disappear.
remember this
before you get
into a relationship.

sometimes,

regardless of how hard you try,

you can't forget someone.

did you ever think

that perhaps you never could,

because you were never meant to?

a relationship involves 2 people,

not 40.

if you want to give this a chance,

ask the entourage to leave.

sometimes

people need to leave your life

in order for you to realize

how important it is

to have them back.

if what you have with your friends

is what you have in your relationship,

then you got it right.

take back

the angry things that you said.

you know you only meant them

in the moment.

it wasn't meant for a lifetime.

don't let them be

the one that got away.

you may be yearning
for someone right now.
but in this moment,
you also have people in your life
who pay attention to you,
who care for you.
remember, that is love, too.

falling in love

is one of life's easiest moments.

relationships take effort, yes.

but loving someone

should feel effortless.

that's when you know

you're with the right person.

the people you love
aren't always within reach -
to be seen, to be heard,
to be touched.
but they can always be felt.

people are going to let you down
from time to time.
you may even let yourself down.
but the goal isn't
to never make a mistake
or be with people who never do either.
you are committed to working on yourself.
fill your circle with people
who are willing to do the same.

the person you love

trusts you.

and that means they trust

that the words you speak to them

are the truth.

that's something

you ought to take seriously.

people leave.

people also come back.

a good relationship

appears so in public,

and actually is one in private.

if the person
you're in a relationship with,
was everything you wanted
for your life,
the people closest to you
would know them.
if they don't - ask yourself why?

it's frightening,

to reach out

to someone you love

when they're no longer

a part of your life.

but this fear is temporary.

having to live without them

for the rest of your life –

that regret is forever.

at the end of the day,
people are simply looking
to be acknowledged,
appreciated, nurtured.
be a source that provides it.

your love should feel whole
even in the bad moments.
and it shouldn't feel
like something's missing
even in the good moments.

it's time to give up on people

who have given up on you.

no, it's not harsh.

you're simply restoring the balance.

being mature doesn't mean
you never have disagreements
with others.
it means you don't bring up
things that don't aid
in the resolution
of those disagreements.

you have yet to let go
at the same time.
this is what pushes a relationship
through its roughest patches -
the fact that one person
is always holding on
when the other
is ready to give up.

darling,

you're so easy to love.

anyone who finds it

difficult to be with you

wasn't made for you.

life can change

in a matter of seconds.

to be angry at the people you love

is a waste of precious time.

if you screwed up, apologize.

if they screwed up, forgive.

the grass on the other side

only seems greener.

the patch you got in front of you

looks good.

learn to appreciate it.

it isn't compromise
if it means having to give up
a part of who you are.
your beliefs, values, morals,
shouldn't have to be abandoned.
what needs to be abandoned
are the people making you feel
as if you have to let go
of what's important to you.

you are worth it.

anyone telling you otherwise

never will be.

if you have someone
who loves and supports you,
consider yourself blessed.
don't mess it up
because you think
life is more exciting elsewhere.
there's nothing out there for you.
just a bunch of people
wishing they had what you have.

you are so special.

just because one person on this earth

failed to see it,

doesn't mean it suddenly isn't true.

listen with your eyes.
it may be different
from what you're hearing
with your ears.

if you're going to commit
to forgiving someone,
you must let go
of the moments that hurt you.
let go and wipe the slate clean.
re-visiting the pain
will never let you recover from it.

you're allowed to be wrong.
you're allowed to screw up.
the only mistake
you're making
is when you choose
not to own up to it.

at the end of the day,
waiting for an apology
means you're still holding on
to resentment.
if you really want to move forward,
forgive without conditions.

be the first to reach out.

your pride may suffer.

but better your pride

than your relationships.

don't punish people for past mistakes.
they did what they could at that age,
with the experience that they had.
you have to forgive them for that.

no, it's not too late

for an apology.

forgiveness

has no expiration date.

sometimes you have to screw up,

so that you know

what it looks like,

what it feels like,

how it hurts you,

how it hurts others.

so there won't be a next time.

dream

work hard for what you want.
the path of least resistance
has never taken anyone
anywhere that lasts.

too old for that,

don't have enough money for that,

too tired for that,

not strong enough for that,

too stressed for that,

not smart enough for that,

not religious enough for that,

don't have time for that.

throw those excuses out.

you have enough youthfulness,

money, energy, strength, peace,

intelligence, faith, time.

you have enough.

do it all.

who told you it was too late?

they're wrong.

it's never too late.

if you wait to see

what others think

before you make decisions,

then you're living life

on other peoples' terms.

just go for it.

go on, do you.

2 steps forward

and 30 steps back.

you know what that means:

that you only have

28 steps this time

instead of 30

to get moving again.

keep going.

you want to live a life

you're in love with

instead of one

you have to settle for.

what is a bad idea?

something you're sure

will never work,

is not realistic,

or simply out of reach.

but if we look back at life,

some of the best decisions

we've made...

started off as a bad idea.

beautiful things can come
out of another chance.
do yourself a favour –
try again.

if you want something,

go get it.

want to do something?

go do it.

it will always be impossible

so long as you believe

in your own limitations.

have faith

in what you cannot see.

fight for it.

excuses are for people

who don't want it badly enough.

you're on your knees

in sincere prayer,

asking for a sign.

you get one.

you rejoice at its coming.

as the days pass

and nothing becomes of it,

you slowly lose faith.

but remember,

signs never expire,

only your patience does.

don't give up.

you can have what you love,
and do what you love.
believe in yourself
and your dreams
for a change.

a support system
needs only one person
who believes
that you will achieve
all that you set out to achieve.
be a part of someone's dream.

follow your heart.
believe that it will not
lead you astray.
trust yourself for once.

dream big.

don't waste time

thinking about HOW

you're going to get there.

all you need to focus on –

is that you're going to get there.

the path may not have been
what you anticipated.
but the end goal hasn't changed.
still the same dream.
still worth chasing.

just because

it isn't within reach right now,

doesn't mean it never will be.

no one knows

what the future holds.

but why not believe

that it's going to be good?

we often wonder

how long we should fight

for a dream

before we give up on it.

the answer is forever.

hold on... it's closer than you think.

there's no rule that says
once you give up on something,
you can't go back and try again.

when you want it

with your whole heart,

and you do something about it –

the fact that you tried

is something to be proud of.

staying focused
means putting yourself
and your dream
in an impenetrable bubble,
and keeping the people
who don't believe in you
on the outside.

after achieving success,
share with those
who are where you used to be.
no one should understand
the hustle better than you.

do what's right for you.
not everyone is going to be
happy about it.
but you're the only one
who has to deal
with the consequences
of living a life
filled with regrets.

what comes
at the end of patience
is definitely worth the wait.

the minute you've convinced yourself
that something isn't going to work,
you stop looking for a reason
to make it work.
if it means something to you,
never stop looking.

no one is 100% certain

about the big decisions in life.

it's okay to be afraid.

it's okay to be confused.

but don't allow uncertainty

to be the reason

you don't give

something a chance.

they may never see

what you want them to see.

but God sees it.

and He knows you tried.

your world right now
may consist of having to sacrifice
and learning to do without.
but there is beauty
in your present situation.
remind yourself of the potential good
you may reap tomorrow
from the struggles
that you face today.

and what do you do

when you have it all?

you find someone

who has nothing

and you share.

too easily, 'someday' becomes 'never'.

sometimes

there is no good reason to wait.

some moments in life

aren't meant to be saved for later.

trust your gut.

it provides you with insight

that logic never can.

if you have to convince yourself

that this is what you want -

then it's not what you want.

just because you can't see

what's happening,

doesn't mean nothing is happening.

make good money,

live a modest life.

make more money,

help others live the same way.

did you give up too soon?

go – get it back.

that dream

was put into your heart

for a reason.

not so you can continue

with what's safe,

but so

you can take a chance.

about the author

After experiencing the healing power of words, Renuka decided to share her snippets of wisdom with everyone through her popular blog. Guided by her pen, she embarked on a journey to change lives and help others work through their own moments of darkness. Her debut book will undoubtedly extend that power to many, many more. She lives in Toronto, Canada, and continues to update her blog at renukawrites.tumblr.com.

www.ingramcontent.com/pod-product-compliance
Lightning Source LLC
Chambersburg PA
CBHW061821040426
42447CB00012B/2754